OPEN BURNING

OPEN BURNING

Poems by
Christopher McCurry

Accents Publishing • Lexington, Kentucky • 2020

Copyright © 2020 by Christopher McCurry
All rights reserved

Printed in the United States of America

Accents Publishing
Editor: Katerina Stoykova
Cover Illustration: "abbraccio" by Sigrid Thaler
Graphics: upfromsumdirt

Library of Congress Control Number: 2019957669
ISBN: 978-1-936628-61-2
First Edition

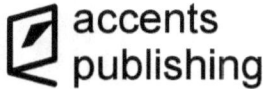

Accents Publishing is an independent press for brilliant voices. For a catalog of current and upcoming titles, please visit us on the Web at

www.accents-publishing.com

CONTENTS

The Epoch of Nothing Beyond Her / 7
A Bit About Rings / 8
Love / 11
The Man Who Was Thursday / 12
Two Arguments / 14
Your Personality / 15
Silent Urban Fringe Noir / 17
Most Mornings / 19
The Name of Your Nail Polish Is Free Spirit / 21
What to Expect / 22
Nostalgic American Period Drama With Korean Othering / 23
| / 24
Girls / 25
Time Travel / 26
Tarantinoesque Societal Underbelly Soap Opera / 27
|| / 29
||| / 30
I Need to Catch You Up On Thirty Years of Subtext / 31
Where I Find Simple Math Useful / 34
Daughter / 35
Surreal Japanese Mumble-Core / 36
A Common Tale of Woe / 37
|||| / 39
Drown Is a Verb / 40
Away From the Windows / 41
𝍷𝍷𝍷𝍷𝍷 / 42
𝍷𝍷𝍷𝍷𝍷 | / 43
𝍷𝍷𝍷𝍷𝍷 || / 44
𝍷𝍷𝍷𝍷𝍷 ||| / 45
𝍷𝍷𝍷𝍷𝍷 |||| / 46
When You Talk to Me / 47
Anger / 48
How It Feels When Your Wife Leaves You / 49

French New Wave Influenced Latin American Apocalyptic ... / 50
Signs of the Approaching Apocalypse / 51
𝍶 𝍶 / 52
The Road This Morning / 53
Open Burning / 54
Daughter / 55
Quirky Family Dramedy / 56
How It Feels When Your Wife Leaves You II / 57
Post Apocalyptic Romance with American Racism / 60
It Seems a Strange Time to Love / 61
How It Feels When Your Wife Leaves You III / 62
Wash This Body / 63
Because You Asked About the Line Between Happy and Sad ... / 65
𝍶 𝍶 | / 66
Dreams in Which I'm Kissing / 67
It Wouldn't Be Fun If the Plane Didn't Crash / 68
Most Nights / 69
PG-13 Superhero Movie / 70
𝍶 𝍶 || / 72
Teaching My Daughter to Survive the Apocalypse / 73
There Won't Be Any More Sonnets But / 74
Bone Brush / 75

Acknowledgments / 77

About the Author / 79

This one, this one's for me.

Talking about dreams is like talking about movies, since the cinema uses the language of dreams; years can pass in a second and you can hop from one place to another. It's a language made of image. And in the real cinema, every object and every light means something, as in a dream.

—Federico Fellini

For love is no part of the dreamworld. Love belongs to Desire, and Desire is always cruel.

—Neil Gaiman, *The Doll's House*

THE EPOCH OF NOTHING BEYOND HER

When she was born my mind went dark.

I no longer dreamt my death.
I craved my unanchored core.

There was no end to the exhaustion,
knowing my teeth were always my teeth

never reabsorbed to gnaw on the hawk's
heart at the end of the rope in my chest.

Four years later on her birthday the dreams return.
I'm locked in a cell and an eye of gray watches me.

In the black of the pupil there's a man with my teeth
eating from the palms of his hands.

A BIT ABOUT RINGS

I couldn't afford a ring.
Your dad gave you one.
The jeweler told us it was fake.

A fake blood red stone, a fake ruby.
I laughed.

A pair of pants that I wear all the time without washing
had a tarnished silver ring in the back pocket. The band
had been molded to spell love. A friend had given it
to our daughter and she had given it to me so she wouldn't lose it.

I wish the following story about my brother weren't true:
Once upon a time he found a wife.
Once upon the exact same time my father opened
a safe and took out a Krugerrand.
My brother had it melted into rings
for him and his wife to wear.
Once upon a time just after
my brother went to the jeweler
with a Krugerrand, that jeweler
had a Krugerrand and my brother
had two rings made of gold.

My nervous habit hasn't stopped.
I thumb where the ring used to be, laugh,
swallow my fist, swallow stones.

How is a heart like a ruby?
Both are red.

Speaking of my brother.
He once gave away an expensive engagement ring
because he felt like god wanted him to.

Because I'm a leftie, I always take my ring off to masturbate,
which we both did. I'm just the one who writes about it.

You never wore your ring. You'd lose it.
Said it bothered you. Said you loved me. Said it didn't mean anything.
Left me. Left your ring.
I gave you mine in a small box.
You gave me forty bucks and a poem you had handwritten the first fight
we had. It said:

You're a Good Man

So I'll fight myself
tooth and nail
to keep you

You taped your ring to the piece of paper.

You asked me not to write any more poems about you.
Or at least not to publish anymore without your permission.

I'm not really sure how this is about rings specifically. But because I wore one in a marriage to you, you felt like you had the right to ask.

In Australia we rewatched the *Lord of the Rings* series because that's what the people renting us the cabins had behind the counter.

When you went out at night with your friends you'd compromise by wearing a ring that wasn't your wedding ring. I said it didn't matter either way. It turns out it really didn't.

The other day I took our daughter shopping for a birthday present. I bought her a mood ring at the register because she had never had one. Her ring turned orange. Orange, the small informational card said, meant she was anxious. She wanted to know when she would be calm. When she would be happy.

LOVE

a sack
of boulders
knocking over
your shoulder
bruise your
spine
wriggle in
the ache
it's a slow
heal but
the dogs
won't dig
up the meat
anymore
now that the
stones rest
on top.

THE MAN WHO WAS THURSDAY
after G.K. Chesterton

fell in love
with a girl
who was Saturday.

She fell in love
with his falling
in love with her

Saturday boobs and her
Saturday laugh and her
Saturday way of not caring

that he was Thursday
because she liked
for the moment

his Thursday glasses and
his Thursday bedtime and
his Thursday sized salary

that he spent on her
until she almost loved
Thursdays. That and

he was so nearly Friday
that sometimes she would
forget that he would never

have cocky certainty
or casual wear
or pizza nights

and sometimes he would
forget, too, and they
were happiest then.

TWO ARGUMENTS

First she calls me
dumb then says
let's have a baby.

What I know now
that I didn't then
is she's saying

she's afraid I love
her less each day.
It is hard to rely

on facts. We have
exactly two kinds
of spaghetti sauce

in the fridge and
three types of noodles
in the cabinet.

YOUR PERSONALITY

After Katerina Stoykova

For five years I've been trying
to give you the swiss army knife
you'll need for this fucked up life.

Sharp, serrated, capable of shearing,
a corkscrew for celebrations,
tweezers and toothpick for smaller problems.

With it you'd lightsaber
your way through school,
though I know the toolkit

of the standard swiss army knife
doesn't come with that or a halberd
even if you'll need both of those

and the world's most compact blowtorch
and the slingshot I used all my life

because much was greater than me
but with it I learned to be unafraid.
These you'll need, and there will never be

a good time to tell you why
to tell you that men will want
to rape you that men will want

to cage and burn your body
if you refuse. And why
when you are afraid of me

I think good
wish me dead—

what's more useful

to a little girl
than knowing
men are dangerous.

SILENT URBAN FRINGE NOIR

Nameless dark haired boy works nights
on the edge of the city in the last place
in town you can buy books from the rack.

The only light is neon. A group of teens
come in, loud and out of place—they
knock a stand of comics to the ground.

She helps him pick them up. He thinks
her body is like a dolphin's. They stand
next to each other staring at the shit

job they've made of their lives and rack
of comics. He goes home with her to her
house that's several small houses tucked

inside one another. The group of friends
is already there and drunk or high and
the two of them sit close to each other

and the camera cuts to them wrapping
their skin in black cloth bodysuits
with mesh over her breasts and ass

and on his a rubber sling for his dick
the head of which is a pink faced bear
smiling with round ears. The film cuts

again to rubbing, the bear's head bouncing,
and then they are running through the house
within the houses, and we are to understand

that they are in love with who they want
to be but can't. Cut again. They are in her
parents' closet sitting underneath the suits

her father wears to work, hiding behind
his shoes as he gets ready for work.
They sleep there all day. Cut to the back seat

of a taxicab where the boy is riding alone.
In his mind she arches her body
and her smooth stomach rises to his mouth.

MOST MORNINGS

I wake up hungry
which isn't a metaphor

for there are things in this life
I want but don't have.

I want to eat. Bananas,
leftover pot roast, a fist

full of gummy bears,
but I don't because

I'm trying to listen
when I'm spoken to.

I hear the self tastes
like a big bowl

of marshmallow-only Lucky Charms,
a steak from my dad's grill,

a tomato pulled from an extra mayo,
extra bacon BLT. Often it's cool water

flowing over boulders as
smooth as shoulder blades.

I'm reminded of the first choice
each morning to take in your hands

the small pump of your heart and inhale.

If you forget the body
is practiced, the body

remembers to keep
itself alive, patiently

waiting for you to hook
your fingers in your mouth.

THE NAME OF YOUR NAIL POLISH IS FREE SPIRIT

First day of second grade
and we are both still learning

if there's too much
it will spill over.

Too little and you have
to paint a second coat.

You say mom is really
good at painting

your nails. You tell me
she can paint designs.

I'd like to be as good
as her one day, I say.

I'm going to have to practice.
I use a Q-tip to clean

the edges. You smudge
the pinky. I dab the bristles

to fill in a hole. You tell me
I'm doing a pretty good job.

The polish matches your dress
for tomorrow. You go to bed

with your hands steepled.
You're afraid. It looks like prayer.

WHAT TO EXPECT

I tell people that every morning
I'm certain you will be dead.

That until I feel your chest rise,
hot breath on the tips of my fingers,

I'm bereft. It's been like this
since your birth. Half blind

and desperate, shaking you,
saying your name, calling your name

as if you've just sprinted over a rise
but could still be within earshot.

Fear has a sharp knife, I tell people.
You're the whetstone, the honing rod.

NOSTALGIC AMERICAN PERIOD DRAMA
WITH KOREAN OTHERING

The problem is easy to identify
but impossible to overcome.

We have agreed to buy four
houses and can't afford them.

There's a matchbox, thin-walled house
just like the one you grew up in,
but not the exact one. It doesn't
smell enough like bleach.

An airy eighteenth-century house
with not-quite-unripe-banana green carpet,
chandeliers every couple of steps, and
sitting rooms, more sitting rooms than
there are any other type of room.

Then there's this Richie Rich sort of half
loft, half Chucky Cheese house with
impractical walls and other people's kids.

The house you like the most is the one
that looks like ours but the ceiling
leaks and water bulges the walls out.
Of course it costs the most but you have a plan.

The Korean child who silently follows
you has a tiny blade she paints white
and stamps across her top lip before
leaving to avenge our lost dignity
and who knows what else in her past.

I

You ask me if you look stupid
and there's no doubt in my mind
the answer is yes. And it is
such a relief to find you grateful
that we hug each other and are
happy. Truth, for once, doesn't turn
us rabid in a room overexposed
with light and nowhere to lay
but a cold metal slab. It's true
what they say. They cut off
the head to test for rabies in animals.
That's the only way to know before
the symptoms show and
you're thirsty but scared of water.

GIRLS

I'm watching this show
where people kiss each other
without asking the other person
if they want to kiss
and these kisses say everything
they haven't been saying for like
three episodes. Surprise,
articulate kisses
that I'm not having
and have never had
because I'm socially awkward
and when I want to say something
that's hard to put into words
I usually say nothing
or go home and think about
the best way to say it or
think about if I even really want to say it at all or
think about how I can say something else
that could maybe be construed for what I want to say
which is usually
I would like it
very much
if I could kiss you
until we both shake
with want.

TIME TRAVEL

She's starting to look more like you now.
I'm grateful for the five years I hung around
in her face. I wonder how you feel that even
that subtle reminder of me is fading. Tonight,
I brushed her hair back behind her ear while
she slept and thought about how you would
look when she wears my scowl or that fishhook
of a smile I wore to pull you in. I couldn't imagine
disgust, but I tried to get as close as I could.
It is tough to be elided is what I'm trying
to say. Like shouting underwater or making a
fist when you first wake up. I should have brushed
your hair back over your ear, should have been a fool
more, should have forgotten myself, been a forest
or a sea, stopped trying to be and just faded into is.
I do know this—it will be nice to see you
in the morning as you sit at the breakfast bar,
fingers sticky with syrup, hair wild again like
nothing I do to it even matters. For a moment
it will subdue itself but no vow will be kept
when I walk away and leave it too long by itself.

TARANTINOESQUE SOCIETAL UNDERBELLY SOAP OPERA

You accept the invitation
to an abandoned storefront
beneath high-rise apartments.

The awning is white
with a blue stripe.

Inside men mill about
a dead body. Someone
puts a gun to your face
to explain no one
is allowed to leave.

It takes a long time
to cut the skull off.
They remove the brain,
the arms, the legs.

The lighting grows rusted and hazy.

The theory is this:
the more of you
from different parts
of life involved,
the harder it will be
for the police.

You will each take a piece
of this man with you.

The man with the gun
convinces you by firing
a bullet through the eye
of someone who was
not yet convinced.

As you all leave the building
carrying your sack, a woman,
the man's wife, wails
like she knows exactly
what each of you carries.

The man was a doctor.
Important. Famous.
He owed people money.

There is the impression
that you were supposed
to have had longer to get away.

In the airport a woman leans
over and tells you, you really
should be running—they will pin
this on whoever they catch
and everyone loves a good
story about a teacher fucking
up his life. It will be front page news.

II

As if a vacation looms you pack
your clothes, find a drawer that could
use sorting and make a mess of it.
Here's a task, a small pile you will
have to focus on straightening.
You'll leave trash strewn on the floor
and I will come behind and pick it up.
There's humor in this, like how you
call the sex we are having an exit tax.
Tonight when you come you cry out
and I do too as though together we conjure
a new reality out of pleasure, a new present,
one that's simpler to walk away from
but also easier to return to.

III

She wants to know why you have to move
and I wouldn't tell her you don't have to.

I tell her there's a you in your mind
you are anxious to meet.

She'll have your laugh
and your comfy slippers on.

You'll sit on the couch with a cup of tea
and look inside and say hello
to yourself, give yourself a hug.

It's been awhile since you've seen her, I say.

I don't know what to say to her next question:
But what if you're not happy?

So I tell her I think you and she will be.
And if not, you both can come back home.

I NEED TO CATCH YOU UP ON THIRTY YEARS OF SUBTEXT

You are baking a cake. It is chocolate with bright red raspberries on top.

Don't worry. It's fine.
I don't really need one. I just want one.

For a while we house trained our god.

When I left my mother's house I left
on the dresser a small teddy bear with perfumed hair.

It's going to rain.

That summer I stayed at your house so much the lamp in the cage
sucked all the moisture out of the lizard's body.

Why don't you ever tell me anything about your life?

Gray sweatpants. Gray sweatpants. Gray sweatpants.
Gray sweatpants. Gray sweatpants. Gray sweatpants.
Gray sweatpants. Gray sweatpants. Gray sweatpants.

There's 200 gallons of water in the crawl space.
The air conditioner fan is stuck.
The gas has been cut until we find the leak.

Forgive me Father for I have sinned.

Once there was a man who had a wife but that man liked the sandwich
made by someone who was not his wife—they all survived.

We kept the dogs we had in a cage in the backyard and
fed them twice a day.

And then, you'll never believe what happened next, he cried.

You wore a white dress with red roses and a high collar to my first grade birthday party. Teenage Mutant Ninja Turtle birthday cake.

It's not that the bottle fit. It's that she don't give up trying.

What I want most is someone to talk storms with.

Pizza for lunch the day the World Trade Center came down.
My juice box wrapped in tinfoil so the brown paper bag doesn't tear.

What's the deal with leaving the front door open and the TV on?
Don't you know it's too late to leave with that suitcase, dad?

If what we are about to do is safe, why does she wear gloves and have to test the batteries?

I do.

My god, my god, why have you forsaken me?

You wore jean shorts and a bikini top and
loved the water slides at Kings Island.

We didn't expect the crawdad to live even if he was the biggest
one any of us had ever seen.

My hamster ate the heart of my brother's hamster.

I made a necklace out of it.

You get up and leave and that's it—
except for the memory of your long legs and your blue underwear.

We decided not to go to the pool that day because the cat flopping in the driveway with half its head missing made us all sick to our stomachs.

I was asked not to let them kill her, and I let them.

Sometimes when I dream I think I am lightning and then I am.

She's in your lap and the fire slow to start at first eventually pushes us further away from its blaze.

WHERE I FIND SIMPLE MATH USEFUL

Let's say you have a kid and that kid rearranges who you are—once there was a boy and now there is still a boy but also the idea of a man. Let's say your father tells you that a kid is a baby goat and you don't disagree with him. Let's say you nearly die in Ecuador and you come home a month early because already this baby goat has been a baby goat for six months and was a baby goat for two months before anyone ever even knew about it. Fucking baby goats. And now let's say you had from the moment it was born into this world approximately eighteen years before it was a full grown goat. And that's roughly six thousand five hundred and seventy days and the man you want to be to this baby goat is the kind that's there every single one of those days because your own father was not but still somehow thinks that it is important not to call your unborn child a kid because a kid is a baby goat. And let's say that now there's an agreement that says you'll only be there for your kid half of that time or three thousand two hundred and eighty-five days or out of every year only one hundred and eighty-two point five days and it's not like on those days you will be any more the idea of the man you want to be for not having been there on the others—you'll still be distracted and hate doll play and burn the waffles and be frustrated with your baby goat for not listening. Let's say you'll never be the man you wanted to be and you don't know what to call yourself now and math can't help you with that but it can prove it to be true in its own cold way.

DAUGHTER

I think I have invented you when
I call your name and you don't respond.

In each room there are effigies
nailed to the wall. You dressed in

school clothes. You meditating
on a rock in the middle of the river.

You holding onto a sundial that says
grow old with me, the best is yet

to be. The mind is a half-dumb beast.
Without your voice it does not believe

you exist. It threatens to rout the life
I've built. But then I see you through

the window, sitting on top of the car
in a crouch waiting for our friends to arrive.

You're practicing Tae Kwon Do. Earlier
you told me that just because you're

alone doesn't mean you're lonely.
Even though I'm glad I didn't make

you up inside my head, I also can't
fathom how you came to be. Maybe

you can't either and that's why you pick
the blister in the center of your palm

and say to everyone when they arrive,
look, look at this, it's my skin. It's coming off.

SURREAL JAPANESE MUMBLE-CORE

Watching a Tri-fente™ match
a man in a white shirt
with the Friendship™ logo
impales his opponent then winks
at you. You turn to leave

but come back and it's the same
moment except the man in the white
shirt willingly jumps on his own
Tri-Fente™ killing himself. Now you know
this means you have to die, too.

So you run—a large man with a red
Tri-fente™ bursts out of a door
in a long hallway with green walls
and you cut down a set of stairs.

More people begin to chase you.
They would like to kill you.
It's a game show. It's televised.
Your fear is everyone's fear.

The building has turned into a corporate
lounge / office area where people
are more relaxed and make their own hours.

There are others here who must die.
You all sit on the couch and talk about
the meaning of monogamy and trying to survive.

A COMMON TALE OF WOE

We are hungry
so we order a pizza
but it won't arrive
quickly enough so
we go and get it.

But one regular
pizza is not enough
so we get deep dish
with bread sticks
and a two-liter.

And we can't wait
until we are home
to start eating
so we take out
a slice in the car.

Enough to coat
the fingers in grease
to spread it along
the steering wheel.

We are no longer
hungry when we sit
down at the table
but we eat anyway.

Nothing will be saved
for later.

Where there is desire
there is excess.

Where this is excess
there is waste.

IIII

I won't survive when I'm no longer
all that impressive to you.

Fellas, I'll say to the guys at the YMCA,
she no longer believes I'm a god.

Rather than comfort me, they'll turn
their heads, ashamed of me for voicing
what they've known or feared all along.

Give these men lightning bolts? Have them
walk on water? What songs have they sung?

Just last night while you slept, our cat,
the heartless one, brought in a bunny,

a baby with the smallest ears. It panted
in the corner, scared and wet. I tried

to save it but I was too slow. The sound,
as it is carried off into the night, hurts the most.

DROWN IS A VERB

I
let
you
sink
in
to

when your arms give out
and your legs kick wide
and your eyes ask me
if this is what you had planned
why the sunscreen, why the goggles
why the well-balanced meals
why the eight o'clock bedtime and
why ever get cranky with me at all.

You cry and shake and say you thought
you were going to die and I say no
that wasn't death that was drowning.

It's what we do when there's no one to lift us up and out of the water.

AWAY FROM THE WINDOWS

This time a tornado. This time the plan
is to hide in the hallway bathroom.

This time we have no choice but to wait—
to watch. I used to hunker down, my head
tucked near my knees against the wall
heaving, the heavy-knuckled clouds
cracking as they clenched into fists.

I was much older than you and scared of storms.

You and I will take pillows and some blankets,
a flashlight, my phone. You'll lie down in the tub,
I'll cover you up. I'll try to act like I'm not afraid
so that you aren't afraid. I'll read to you.

You want to know if we all go to the same place.

Not when we die but when the tornado sets us
down in our house. Because I won't lie to you about death:
that's not how this works. The wind rips the house apart.
You're crushed or beaten or impaled by flying debris.
Hence the blanket. Hence the pillows. Why not cover
me with something hard, you ask. That's not a bad idea
I say. Because I will lie to protect the tiny hope
every one of us harbors against death.

Later that evening, you want to know
why a car kills you when it runs you over.

This time I tell you how we can't help but to build
what we can't control and sometimes that ends you
and sometimes it helps bring you to a place you've never been.

||||

We need a new way to talk about our bodies
during sex. Murder wears me out. I don't want
to pound you, take you from behind, tear it up.

Knocking the bottom out sounds to me like
hitting speed bumps in a CVS parking lot
while going too fast. The carriage of the car

slapping the asphalt, tossing whatever's
in the trunk around. I don't want to hit it.
Or beat it up. I've never plowed anything

or ridden something that had a choice
in the matter. If I say that I want to bone you,
please say eww, what the fuck. Same goes

for smash and screw. Let's start with this:
your clit under my tongue and name it.

卌 |

Is everything alright?   Everything is fine.
Would you like me to hold your hand
while you fall asleep?   That's okay.
Are your feelings hurt because I didn't
think you would care or because I didn't
think about you at all?   Is there really a difference
in the end?   This is the end then?   You want
me to say goodnight?   Yes. Please.
The light in the kitchen is on, I'll turn it off.
Are you coming back to bed?   Is that what
you want—do you want me to?   Do you
really have to ask?   Right now I need to know.
I want you to come back.   That's all
you had to say.   That's all you want to hear.

𝍫 ||

It's true I love her more than you.
If such a thing can be measured in sound,
the accordional body, feet pattering
through the kitchen, the bellow of her lungs.
Every night I listen to her heart compressing.
The streetlight outside our apartment
as she sleeps next to you pours through
her and projects on your skin the cities
she'll build, the men and women she will love.
My death. Your death. Her own. I know you
to do the same. Count each breath,
take stock of scent. Milk and spit and moldy
peach. Every sigh from her upturned face
replacing me just as I replace you, in part, in half.

~~IIII~~ III

Neither of us has killed the other so far.
The tools of misery are slow:
a half a turn of the vice, one drop
of battery acid. Used to be we'd
agree on terms and then our weapon
of choice. We'd meet at the appointed
time on hallowed ground to bludgeon
and slash, try to shove a finger in the mouth
and rip the cheek back over the teeth.
We'd adhere to the rules of puncture.
And after stitch ourselves up. Take flame
to the wound. Drive out infection.
How do we recover from this? The hole
in my gut, blood leaking from your ear.

//// ////

If after twenty-nine years this marriage ends
and you move out with some of your stuff
but some you leave behind because we've
forgotten what is yours and what is mine,
I will think of you in your new apartment
with another man's mouth on your nipple.
Even if you say it's not like that—not about that.
I will think of you as floating through the rooms
much lighter without me. And what kind
of man will I be? Rag picker of memories.
I will imagine myself the suffering one.
That's it, I know. Or I think will be it. Poor me,
failed to lift you up? Insisted you needed help?
Am I getting close? Do you know? Please, tell me now.

WHEN YOU TALK TO ME

I want you
to think
I'm listening

just like

you want me
to think

you love me.

ANGER

a line
cast
and
weighted
bait
slicking
the hook
yank it
through
the meat
in the
mouth.

HOW IT FEELS WHEN YOUR WIFE LEAVES YOU

What is the word *my* but a sack
of a creature with one wiggling tooth
we sink into one another.

I'm a man gasping in a paper bag
blown wide open at the bottom.

We put such faith in flimsy things.

I can't sleep.

At times I feel ugly. At other times a chunk
of startling blue ice rived and swallowed by the sea.

I feel unwanted. Unlovable.
And so goddam ridiculously dumb.

I want to hide my face so the babysitter
doesn't know what a chainsaw
her body is to the pulp of me.

Intermittently, distant places I've never
been seem more like home than here.

I can't sleep because I'm afraid I'll forget
to remind myself to breathe.

When I find something she's left behind
it feels like a former self she's grown out of.

To yammer, to wail, to yowl, to bay, to bellow,
to scream, to bawl, to keen, to open the windows
so someone might hear, but leave the doors locked.

I can't sleep but I want to feel safe.

FRENCH NEW WAVE INFLUENCED LATIN AMERICAN APOCALYPTIC LOVE STORY

We have boxes of dead soldiers' belongings.
In one a copy of *The Brothers Karamazov*.
Another stuffed with letters and flowers.

Our job is to bury the boxes because we can't bury the bodies.

There are long scenes of us just being what we are.

Humans digging up the earth.
Humans smoking hand-rolled cigarettes.
Humans fucking up and dropping the boxes

off the back of the truck so we don't know which
photograph goes with which box. Who had a baby
and who had a girl they called baby.

The drive back from the graves is through the mountains.

The first bomb lands behind us deep in the valley.
It could be the sun setting, the way the light flares
in the rearview mirror, next to your smile.

We think we can outrun them. What's foolish
is the hope that each explosion will be the last.

One hits the mountain and melts the car
and at first we don't understand
that the car is melting into us and we are melting too,

and when I do, I see my lover and me.

We are the handsomest we've ever been
lying together in a yellow tent. It's a dream.
Another bomb above us rains down molten rock.
See, he tells me, you didn't feel a thing.

SIGNS OF THE APPROACHING APOCALYPSE

The birds begin   to look   like drones

      in the distance.

The drones begin   to look like finally

      I'm not afraid.

We bought a bed

      too big for me to reach

            out and touch

            the valley of your back.

At the first sign

      of heat you say

oh no, not you.

There were mountains   here once.

|||| ||||

You go to bed early with a headache.
I jerk off and feel guilty, so I sweep the kitchen
and then the dining room. My body at work
wakes you and I hear you ask the dark
Who is it? well? who's there? You're dream
drunk and don't hear, when I say no one.
In the morning, the counters and table will be clean,
the air won't reek of what we've thrown away.
And I'll be gone, after drying the last dish,
wiping down the grease collected on the range,
tossing out expired coupons still stuck to the fridge,
still reminding us of the past, its cheap wants.
You won't miss me. We don't
mourn what needs to be mopped up.

THE ROAD THIS MORNING

the thunderstorms
the who are you again / oh yes my wife
the hours we talk
the people / everyone we think we know / must be losing their minds
the turning right around because I forgot
the hours / really just trees / really just houses / really just more roads
the more who are you / oh yes fellow travelers
the rain the plain red pink of your cheek in the heat
the air conditioner broken
the hours of silence
the and and and / and and and of tires
the song you sing still in my head
the ankles / your ankles disappearing into the rest station
the way your mouth hunts
the hours we are younger
the because because / because because of the wipers
the excuse you / who are you again / oh yes my husband / oh yes
the pulling over on the shoulder
the now / now of cars going seventy
the hands now everywhere
the hours of skin on your back
the hours / the hours / the hours
the signs no longer making sense
the at last / we are here and finally stretched out next to each other
the rain tapping the hotel window / please please please / please please

OPEN BURNING

An apocalypse should be sudden
and personal like the snare

in the cord of your spine
at last yanked

and accounted for.
By now at least one theory

has to be right. I'll see you,
love, disintegrated.

The question is not
how will the world end,

but what will we do
until it's our turn

to toss our bodies
in the burn barrel?

DAUGHTER

If tucked
like black opal
somewhere
in the body's
carmine
is a soul,
leave it be.

It's a useless
thing. No trinket
for a chain.

You can do
so much more
with your hands
than worry
a small stone.

QUIRKY FAMILY DRAMEDY

You work at a gas station and I live on the second floor. Your boyfriend grills the roller dogs, the cheese stuffed hot dogs, the tornados. I had to come downstairs for napkins. Our daughter had spilled ketchup on her leggings. You'd just opened. The world needs its Funyuns and Five Hour Energy Drinks. They wonder why I stroll around in my underwear holding a child. I wonder if my dick looks small which isn't as vain as it sounds if you recall the boyfriend near the rolling meat, the spinning brats, his bald head peeking around the grease-streaked plastic protective case. He's a useful type guy. He's a cool guy. I heard your dad say to him, "Hey Fella" like it was a name tag he could reuse. This wasn't in the dream. It was at our daughter's seventh birthday party. Back upstairs in my dream apartment I find a cabinet in an adjoining conference room that has a stack of brown napkins—so I really didn't need to go down to your gas station in the first place.

HOW IT FEELS WHEN YOUR WIFE LEAVES YOU II

Because people like a scab they ask.

I forget to remind myself to think of answer.

I want to sound convincing.

I want them to be satisfied
with what they peel back.

I miss being married. I miss
the woman I married.

The other day she spoke
and I didn't hear what she said.

I said, what did you say, hon?

It had been a year since she left
and we began amputating
pieces of each other—every word
a tooth in the saw of our conversations.

I sometimes say it feels like constantly
having somewhere to be but
being unable to get there.

Like I'm going to be late for work.

Or just remembered that I left
an infant in a car two hours ago
in the baking, treeless parking lot.

These are my recurring dreams.

Other times I'll say my mother used
to lock us out of the house
when we were younger.

Not once when I pounded on the door
did I consider that she was locked inside.

Depending on who asks, I won't say anything,
the clean red blood that follows says enough.

Like I haunt my own life.
Like the magician forgot to put my lower half back on.

Other times I say it's not the end of the world,
which is my own private joke. The punchline:
it was the end of mine. You're talking to a man
with a stick scratching in the dirt, waiting to die.

A slight to mild exaggeration.

For instance, I didn't even try to stop her
from leaving, and evidence suggests I could have
at least tried to stop my wife from leaving—could have
said I love you—don't leave—instead of I won't stop you.

What oozes out is a philosophy
of love tacked behind the bathroom door
in the house where I grew up.

It said, if you love something set it free.
If it comes back to you, it's yours. If not,
it never was.

Problematic, unsound logic—which
is why it's fitting I mostly contemplated
it while taking a shit. Until now.

One response I haven't tried is the classic
answer the question with a question.

Have you ever been the worst part of someone's life?

Could you easily articulate in a brief conversation with an acquaintance how hard it is to unknow a person?

Ever had a scratch you couldn't itch?

Ever reached out to touch someone who was just there, but now has turned and walked away?

POST APOCALYPTIC ROMANCE WITH AMERICAN RACISM
(Set in what used to be Pigeon Forge)

The beginning is chaos.

We set up camp in the woods with extended family.

A black person in a bubble coat is foraging for berries on a path.

This unnerves your mother-in-law even though
we are all just trying to survive.

We are forced to leave the camp. We come upon a native village.

I wonder how anyone can be native to the end of the world.

Let's just say they had embraced living as something active,
done in the present, while we still clung to our relation to the past.

Their leader is a young woman with an arrowed body and painted face.
White triangles under her eyes and red smeared across her forehead.

We are not doing well, and you give me to this woman,
demand I go to her room to mate with her.

I'm hesitant but the world has ended so I see it as a gift.

You die when a rival village slaughters and burns everyone
but me and this woman.

I have to learn the ways of a wild land and a savage woman's
heart once again.

IT SEEMS A STRANGE TIME TO LOVE

I try to tell you
I'm not ruined

but what I say
comes out all

sunken ship

all sand
eroded
statue.

HOW IT FEELS WHEN YOUR WIFE LEAVES YOU III

It might help to know that there are two dreams I keep having.

There's blood on the tips of my fingers. It's from your ear.
You've razored through the cartilage on accident.
You look surprised, but also like you knew what you were doing.

In the house I grew up in my dad stretches out on the floor and I lay down next to him and he holds me and I cry and he doesn't say shit about it.

WASH THIS BODY

I think not. It is summer
and I've just made love
to the woman I love
who is willing to lie
down with me and
not turn her nose up
too much even though
I don't shower often
these June days
and still she laughs
when I run one finger
nail up her spine
and say nonsense
things as men do
when they are jaw-
smacked with love
as I am and it smells
of such earth, which
to me is alive and
fecund and oily and
sick-sticky being
together this way knowing
what has happened
and what is happening
and will happen again
and again and again
and reminds me of how
she says sometimes
she feels more like a man
than a woman and how
I say that must be why
our sex is so goddamn good

because a younger me
loved a hammer grinned boy
and more than a few men
keep room in my heart and
O the stink of ceaselessly
being and potential of every
time I open the door of my
arms to them and they to me
to doing what feels right
and radical like we have done
this morning only I know
far less dangerous but that
is why I go through the day
with a little risk on my lips
and my body reeking like boy.

BECAUSE YOU ASKED ABOUT THE LINE BETWEEN HAPPY AND SAD AND I SAID I'M NEITHER I'M JUST BLAH AND I SAID DOES THAT MAKE SENSE AND YOU SAID YES

After Howard Nemeroc

For Abra

I am decades old pavement
having been trodden on, beaten
down by rain. Hot then cold
and cracked and chipped
and slapped with quickcrete
but still here, still riding up
over that hill and hugging
that turn to the courthouse
and wearing my holes like
inside each one is a seed
winged from a tree, perfect
shelter for some small
creature's desperate meal.

𝍦 𝍦 |

When you're gone too long I begin to build
a life without you. The heart wants a stone

wall eight feet tall to start. The hands want
strips of shopping bags to shape a nest

on the porch where the ear meets the skull.
This will not be a living to be proud of.

I can do nothing to deny my feet their seeking,
my cock its dumb boarish snout its snooping.

Without you I've made a hammock of my spine.
Everything will be temporary cardboard cutouts,

loose screws. This zoo of origami animals is stupid
I know, but the mind craves a complex system

of clean folds, straight lines, of angles so sharp
they make of your absence the absurd neck of swan.

DREAMS IN WHICH I'M KISSING

people I shouldn't be kissing
most frequently the babysitter
a close second my ex-wife
after that a work colleague
a girlfriend from college.

Somewhere in my mind
a channel is stuck on what if.

What if there's more to learn from lips?
What if hate sweetens the tongue?
What if infidelity bites back?
What if nostalgic love is the safest kind of love?

IT WOULDN'T BE FUN IF THE PLANE DIDN'T CRASH

When I finally understood
you were reliving a memory
of your first time flying,
I watched your hand take off
and your mouth form
the percussion of engines.
Then, mid-flight, the airplane
turned into a helicopter
and the whomp of the blades
whirred from your lips as it crashed
like the many times you were
hoisted on my feet, and for fun,
suffered a similar tragedy.
I'm struck now, not by the power
or clarity of your recollection,
but how you told a story
and it was one of dying
and I had taught it to you.

MOST NIGHTS

Cold cracks the bones of the house.
The furnace rubs its hands.
I lay in bed and the dark wants
me to forget myself. I've got teeth
loose in this world in bejeweled jars
with purple felt. White lace gloves
that no longer fit. The haints of former
pets have shook their stones.

Sleep used to be safe but now
the dreams come, cinematic and terrible
in their invention. They say I'm sick.
They say I'm hung from a tree—my feet
in blocks of concrete in the cold lake of this life.
They say I'm stuck here. Last night I
started my job as a Kroger employee,
learning how to bag. A man with no money
tried to steal groceries. I smashed
his face on the ground and told him
he could have asked me for help.

That's the way it is with me.
Violence before compassion.

Because next time I won't be there
but maybe my voice will be
and that's close enough.

Or so I tell myself these nights
in bed with too many layers on
because I'm cold and alone—
wishing someone would show me
how to be me again so I wouldn't
have to do it all by myself.

PG-13 SUPERHERO MOVIE

It's a normal enough day
before the attack. I'm watching
my daughter play with her
friend Kennedy at her school.

I've got an important job,
the kind where I get called
away from what really matters
to ride in the backseat of a car

and talk on the phone and
have two bodyguards with their
stone faces on either side and
the music (layered on in editing)

is full of bass before the bombs
drop and the car flips and I'm thrown
from it as buildings crumble
and flames catch and light

everything up. In the next shot I'm
broken on the ground like I've been burnt
to ash but for my head, and a bald man

with light blue eyes in a suit shoots
me to make sure I'm dead.

But I'm not—the bullet fires back (yes,
from my head) and knocks him flat
and I rise from the pile naked
but whole, glowing red. I'm the Phoenix,

resurrecting is what I do. And that same
energy I use for rebirth I can channel
into others so I use it to break this man more.

He doesn't stay broken. His bones
like centipede legs ripple along
under his skin. Other men who
look just like him join him.

I know now I must find my daughter
because what's the point of all this
fake destruction if there's not
anything so fragile it needs to be saved.

||||| ||||| ||

We decided last night that you would leave me.
I'm not as happy about it as I thought I would be.
All the times you spat in my face and I was free

to hate you for it. Free to take our daughter
and live a different life. One with more poetry
and other women, and I'm the best dad in

the history of deadbeats—basically, I have
it all except you. I don't really want any of that
anymore. I don't even want to prepare myself

for you not being here, asleep as you are now
in our bed after we stayed up and talked and
gave ourselves over to pleasure one more time,

free to please one another, everything else let go.
I came twice and you too many to count
and this was always the best part of us so
we said thank you and then finally goodbye.

TEACHING MY DAUGHTER TO SURVIVE THE APOCALYPSE

You may have to shoot a man
in a tarp shuffling down the road
looking for food, looking for shelter.
A limit has been set for compassion
and there will be no exceeding it.
How hard do you make your heart for this land?
Blood tastes like copper wire. Bones make good tools.
Fire is more signal than warmth. You can learn from the face
what you can't from words. Watch your mother.
For this, watch your mother.

THERE WON'T BE ANY MORE SONNETS BUT

there's this five minutes on the mezzanine
of the Opera House, your hand resting
on her left leg and mine on her right
as she watches the ballerinas below.
Pitiful spectacle. Us. The dancers.
They are just beginners and have
that excuse. But us? Why has it been
years since we both touched our
daughter at the same time? We lost
count. Forgot the routine. I don't know
which of us drew our hand away first,
but I know, at some point, the curtain fell,
and every one of us was called to applaud.

BONE BRUSH

Feathering away at the skin over your ribs while you sleep on
top of me still so small as to be barely here—not like a house
or a tree. Sometimes you hide and the only way I can find
you is your eventual desire to want to be found. I imagine
I'm sweeping away even that to the small braid of your being—
in you a meaning I'm eager to grasp for both our sakes since
you've been asking and telling me how afraid you are to die.
I tell you what I've heard and what I hope is right, that you will
live a long life and death will be careful with you, not painful,
slowly eroding you, untying the bow that anchors you here,
a slow drift across a sky you find friendly and expectant.

ACKNOWLEDGMENTS

All my gratitude to the following people who deserve to be named. You've enriched my life and therefore these poems immeasurably.

My family, Abra McCurry, Vicki McCurry, Michael McCurry, Christy Giles, Lindsay McCurry, John and Janelle McCurry, Crystal and David VanMeter, Eloise Lynch, Susan and Mary Lou Stephens, plus all my cousins and nieces and nephews.

My editor and mentor, Katerina Stoykova.

My friends, Andrew Depew, Sylvia Collings, Bronson O'Quinn, Eduardo Ballestero, Venecia Proctor, Maggie Rue Hess, Madison Burt, Holly Ybarrola, Bobby Howard, Courtney Calk, Matt Middleton Liz Prather, Meredith Bernhard, Amanda Wright, Joe Gross, Louise Gash, Leslie Davis, Morghan Fuller, Bianca Bargo, Sue Churchill, Robin Rahija, Kristen Miller, Dave Harrity, Jaria Gordon, Dennis Preston, Philip Corley, Drew Pomeroy, Tina Parker, Doug Self, Audrey Rooney, Hannah LeGris, Jessica Swafford, Mary Allen, Debbie Adams Cooper, tina andry, Eric Scott Sutherland, Jude McPherson, Ron Davis, Crystal Wilkinson, Jay McCoy, Leigh Anne Hornfeldt, Elizabeth Beck, GA Smith, Meadow Smith, Dean Smith, Frank Betkowski, Andrew Abel, Clay Shields, Candace Chaney, Jennifer Beckett, Derek Glenn, Austin Rathbone, Heather and Keith Dent, Jane Mecham, Helen Feibes.

My teachers, Mrs. Blankenship, Mrs. Fields, Mrs. Murphy, Mrs. Sherrow, Mr. Willoughby, Mr. Smith, Mr. Clark. Ms. Welch, Mrs. Gregory, Mrs. Sims, Mr. Mau, Dan Howell, Erik Reece, Gurney Norman, Nikky Finney, Rebecca Gayle Howell, Julia Johnson, Ruth Forman, David Huddle.

The artists who helped make this book possible, Dan Klemer, upfromsumdirt, Sarah Freligh, Maurice Manning, and Sigrid Thaler.

Thank you to the editors and readers of *Appalachian Heritage*, *Still. The Journal*, The LexPoMo Anthologies, *Literary Accents*, and *Rattle* where some of these poems first appeared.

Shout out to the crew at The Carnegie Center, all of the LexPoMo Poets, and the Workhorse Writers.

ABOUT THE AUTHOR

Christopher McCurry grew up right outside of Lexington, Kentucky in the small town of Paris. In the seventh grade he entered one of his poems in a contest and won a medal. He's since lost the medal but still remembers the poem. His poetry has been nominated for two Pushcart Prizes and featured on NPR's *On Point* as a Best Book of 2016 for his chapbook of marriage sonnets *Nearly Perfect Photograph*. A graduate of the Bread Loaf School of English at Middlebury College and a high school English teacher, he spends his time playing board games, skateboarding, and going on adventures with his daughter Abra. In 2015, Christopher co-founded Workhorse, a publishing company and community for working writers. He believes everyone should write poems and that everyone can. You can find him online at *christophermccurry.com* or *workhorsewriters.com*.

www.ingramcontent.com/pod-product-compliance
Lightning Source LLC
Chambersburg PA
CBHW030347100526
44592CB00010B/868